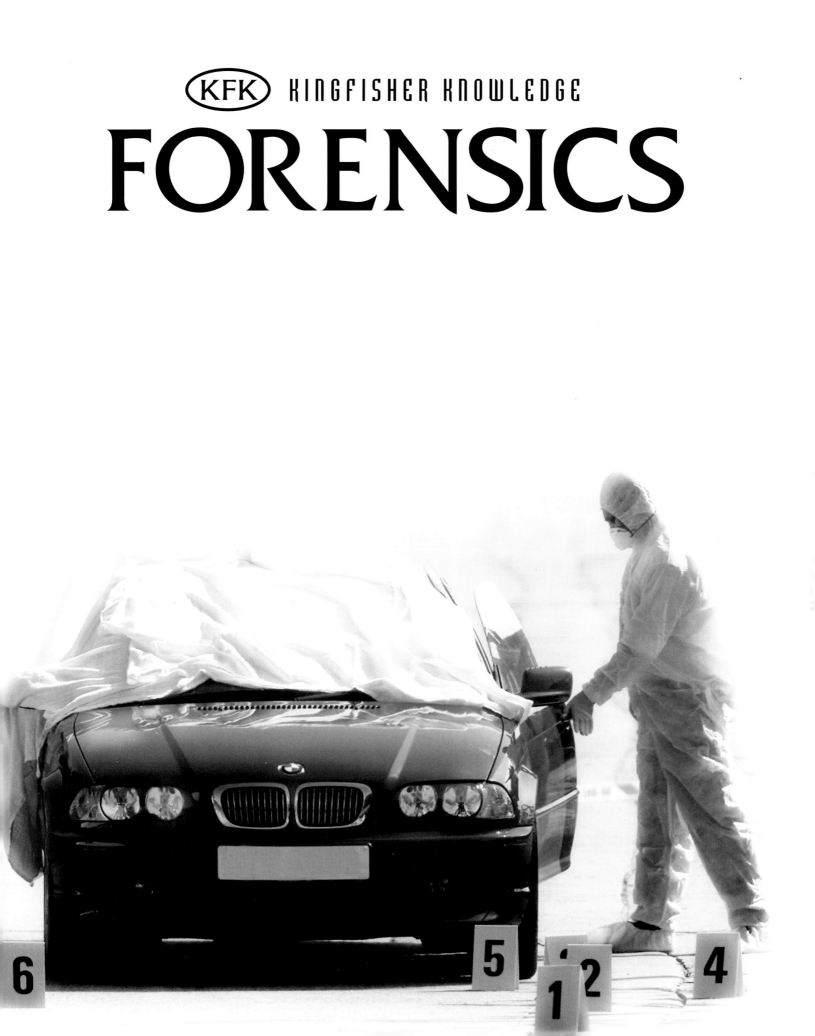

KFK KINGFISHER KNOWLEDGE

FORENSICS

Police officers search a parking lot for evidence after a shooting. To ensure that nothing is overlooked, the police have formed a line, standing shoulder to shoulder. Each officer then searches the area directly in front of him or her.

KFK KINGFISHER KNOWLEDGE

FORENSICS

Richard Platt

Foreword by
Kathy Reichs

KINGFISHER

BOSTON

Editor: Jennifer Schofield
Coordinating editor: Caitlin Doyle
Senior designer: Carol Ann Davis
Picture research manager: Cee Weston-Baker
DTP manager: Nicky Studdart
DTP operator: Primrose Burton

Senior production controller: Lindsey Scott
Proofreader and indexer: Sheila Clewley
Consultant: Dr. C. H. Steele, Principal Lecturer in
    Forensic Science, London South Bank University,
    England

KINGFISHER
a Houghton Mifflin Company imprint
222 Berkeley Street
Boston, Massachusetts 02116
www.houghtonmifflinbooks.com

First published in 2005

1TR/0605/TWP/MA(MA)/130ENSOMA/F
10 9 8 7 6 5 4 3 2 1

LIBRARY OF CONGRESS CATALOGING-IN-PUBLICATION DATA
has been applied for.

ISBN 0-7534-5862-4
ISBN 978-07534-5862-4

Printed in Singapore

Contents

NOTE TO READERS The web site addresses listed in this book are correct at the time of publishing. However, due to the ever-changing nature of the Internet, web site addresses and content can change. Web sites can contain links that are unsuitable for children. The publisher cannot be held responsible for changes in web site addresses or content or for information obtained through third-party web sites. We strongly advise that Internet searches are supervised by an adult.

GO FURTHER . . .
INFORMATION PANEL KEY:

web sites and further reading

career paths

places to visit

CHAPTER 3
CRIME LAB   39

Foreword

Do you ever watch police shows on TV? Or read mystery stories? Ever think you'd be good at catching the bad guys? If so, this book is just for you!

Contrary to popular thinking, police cases are not cracked by glamour or by razzle-dazzle technowizardry. Nor are they cracked by heroes working solo. Law enforcement relies on careful evidence collection, skilled detective work, and good old science. It is through teamwork that investigators learn what happened at a crime scene and who was there. Forensic scientists make up an important part of every police team.

Forensics is packed with information about forensic scientists. It describes what we do in terms of two broad categories: fieldwork (collecting evidence) and laboratory work (analyzing evidence).

In the early 1900s Dr. Edmond Locard was the director of a police laboratory in Lyon, France. He created a rule that still bears his name. Locard's Exchange Principle says that every contact leaves a trace. That means that every time people meet, touch, or even enter a room, they leave tiny specks of themselves behind, and they carry tiny specks off when they go. Maybe a thread, a dust particle, or even an eyelash. It is those transferred specks that sink the bad guys.

Crime scene investigators go to a crime scene and seal it off. They video and photograph the setting and the victim (if there is one). These men and women are trained to spot Locard's tiny specks and to see patterns between things. They know how to collect and preserve fingerprints, blood, tire tracks, paint chips, or bullet fragments—even that dust particle or eyelash that was left behind!

The crime scene workers take everything that they have collected to the crime laboratory. There each scientist examines something different. Some focus on documents and writing. Some look at tools and weapons, or chemicals and poisons, or bombs and explosives, or DNA and other biological substances.

For many years I have worked at a combination crime and medico-legal lab in Montreal, Canada. I work on the medico-legal side. Our section has a specific task. The "evidence" we examine is the victim. Sometimes our job is to identify a body. Sometimes our job is to figure out how or why someone died.

Like those in the crime lab, the scientists in the medico-legal section also have speciality areas. The forensic pathologist performs autopsies to determine the cause of death. The forensic dentist examines teeth. The forensic radiologist studies X-rays.

I am a forensic anthropologist. I examine decomposed, burned, and mummified bodies and skeletons. I may be asked to determine someone's age, sex, race, and height. I may be asked to look for injuries in their bones. I may be asked to estimate how long someone has been dead or to describe what was done to their body after they stopped breathing.

I love being a forensic scientist. It is rewarding and exciting work. I help families gain peace by providing answers. I help police solve crimes by providing clues. I help prosecutors in court by providing testimonies.

Forensics is a terrific introduction to my world. The chapters and photographs explain what my colleagues and I do at the crime scene and in the crime lab. The book shows just how cool science can be.

Forensic science is a hot topic with the media right now. That won't last, but it doesn't matter. Crime will always be with us. Forensic scientists will always be needed. I hope this book inspires you to join our team.

Kathy Reichs

Kathy Reichs—international best-selling crime writer and forensic anthropologist

CHAPTER 1

Signs of the crime

Every minute of every day criminals are at work. To catch them, police forces rely more and more on forensic science—the science of solving crimes.

Forensic science starts at the crime scene—the place where a crime is committed. There investigators hope to find clues that will lead them to a suspect—someone who may have carried out the crime. They search the crime scene for evidence. This means any object, mark, or pattern that can provide them with information about the crime.

By photographing, studying, and testing the evidence, forensic scientists can link suspects to a crime scene and help prove whether they are guilty or innocent.

The crime scene

Blue lights flash on a dark street. "Police line—do not cross" written on yellow plastic tape flaps between trees. Uniformed figures hold back a curious crowd. Welcome to a crime scene. Police officers and detectives take extra care to preserve crime scenes exactly as they find them—because evidence is fragile, and clumsy feet and prying hands can easily destroy it. Without evidence, it may be impossible to solve a crime and catch the criminals who carried it out.

One and only chance

The first police officers to arrive at the scene of a crime must take a careful look around but avoid disturbing anything that they find. There are very good reasons for this caution and care—the first officers to arrive have a special, once-only chance because they see the crime scene completely fresh and untouched. Very soon their own actions—and those of others—will make changes that can never be undone. For example, just walking across a carpet to help an injured person can destroy the footprints of a fleeing attacker.

Preserving evidence

Crime scene officers must take quick steps to protect and preserve the crime scene. They try to see where criminals could have entered before committing the crime—and how they left afterward. These places may hold important clues, such as the suspect's fingerprints, so it is vital that they remain untouched. Crime scene officers also try to guess where they will *not* find evidence. They will only use these areas to enter and leave the crime scene so that they do not disturb other, more important places.

Securing the scene

Once the crime scene is taped off, there are other simple but essential precautions that officers need to take. They must not eat, drink, or smoke because these activities leave traces that may later confuse investigators. For the same reason, they must not use the telephone or the bathroom if they are part of the crime scene. Sometimes their work forces them to make a change to the crime scene—such as opening a door to enter. If this happens, they make a written note recording that the door was shut when they arrived. Details like this can make the difference between a criminal going to jail and escaping unpunished.

Vital witnesses

For all their careful observation and note taking, officers can never know as much about a crime as someone who actually saw it happen. These witnesses are vital to an investigation. Police race to identify them and make sure that they do not leave the crime scene before being interviewed.

◄ When police officers respond to an emergency call, their first jobs are to care for any victims of the crime, arrest suspects (shown left), and identify witnesses (the people who saw the crime).

▶ The more people who visit a crime scene, the greater the chance of destroying evidence. So an important priority for officers is to keep away reporters, curious neighbors—and even other officials whose visit is not absolutely essential. Uniformed officers do this by surrounding the crime scene with "Do not cross" tape and putting an officer on guard.

▶ All evidence that is found, as well as interviews with eyewitnesses, are logged and recorded in police files. Laptop technology and wireless communication enable officers to access files from police headquarters while at a crime scene. This allows them to cross-reference information quickly and easily.

Collecting evidence

Clues that investigators find at a crime scene can lead them to the criminals who are responsible for the crime. However, a thorough search for evidence is important even when the police officers are certain that they know who did it. Without evidence, it is hard to prove that the suspect was even at the crime scene. And in a court of law a judge or jury may doubt what the police tell them if there is not any evidence. Unless it is certain that suspects are guilty, they cannot be punished.

▲ The index number and description of each piece of evidence are stored on a database. This enables officers to keep track of all evidence.

Crime scene officers

It is the crime scene officers' job to search for, preserve, and record evidence. For example, a broken window might show how burglars entered a house. Blood on the window can help identify them, and fingerprints may match a known criminal's record. However, few crimes are this straightforward. Skilled criminals take care not to leave such obvious clues. Even if the explanation of the crime seems clear and investigators believe that they know who did it, they must still record everything.

Starting the search

Officers begin by searching for evidence that time or weather might destroy—tire tracks in snow, for example. Then they look at the areas that are associated with the crime. For example, in murder cases they search close to the body.

Knowing where to look

Crime scene officers also look in less obvious places. For example, a suspect reaching to take something from a shelf might avoid touching the shelf itself. But because right-handed people unconsciously reach out for support with their left hand, officers look for fingerprint evidence on surfaces to the left.

Looking everywhere

So that they do not miss any details, crime scene officers make sure that their search covers the entire crime scene. In a house they list the rooms and search each one. Outdoors, they might stand shoulder to shoulder and walk forward in a line or start in the center and spiral out to the edges.

Bag, seal, and label

Before evidence is removed, it is photographed (see pages 12–13), and its location is plotted on a plan. Then being careful that it is not altered in any way, it is bagged, sealed, and labeled. A record is made of what has been found, who found it, and where it was found. This log of information grows each time anyone studies or moves the evidence. Called the "chain of custody," it enables officers to prove that nobody has tampered with the evidence.

▶ The detail of the search depends on what the officers are looking for and the size of the crime scene. If it is small, they kneel and search with their fingertips.

Photography

Cameras are probably a detective's most useful tool at a crime scene. With a simple snapshot camera, forensic photographers can make a quick record before anything is disturbed during a search for evidence. However, it is not always as simple as it seems. Sophisticated equipment and special lighting techniques are used to show clues that are invisible to the naked eye. Cameras also capture evidence that is too big to remove from the crime scene, as well as traces that later tests may destroy.

▲ Alphonse Bertillon was the first person to realize that photographs are useless for identification unless they all use the same lighting and angle. Here, Bertillon himself poses for the front and side views of the now standard police "mug shot" that he pioneered.

▼ Special forensic light sources create intense beams of bright colors. Used with special chemicals, these shafts of light make fingerprints stand out more clearly in photographs or reveal blood stains that have been washed away.

First photographs

As long ago as 1843—just four years after the invention of photography—Belgian police began taking pictures of known criminals. In France the chief of criminal identification, Alphonse Bertillon (1853–1914), pioneered the use of photography to solve crimes. He made detectives take pictures in a scientific way, with matching lighting and camera angles in order to make comparisons easier. He also insisted that they include a scale, such as a ruler, so that it was easy to judge the size of objects in the final print.

▲ Including a scale in forensic close-up photographs enables detectives to judge the size of the object in the picture. For fingerprints the size is usually obvious, but for other objects, such as knives, the size is less clear—and very important.

Lining up the picture

Some of Bertillon's ideas are in use today. Forensic photographers still include a scale. They also make sure that the camera is positioned exactly in line with the subject, rather than slanted. These precautions ensure that the camera records the evidence as clearly as possible.

However, the technology and equipment that photographers use has changed. Today they use color pictures, and—with digital cameras or instant film—they can see whether they have the picture they want immediately.

► Whether photographers are using film or digital cameras, the methods they use are similar. A lot of their work consists of making a simple record of the crime scene from all angles. For this they use equipment and methods that are hardly any different from those we use for taking everyday photos.

Taking close-ups

When taking close-ups of evidence, detectives need sharp images with a lot of detail. They often light the scene to make the picture clearer and also include a scale bar. For example, evidence that is raised or pressed into a surface, such as tire tracks in mud, is not always easy to see. Placing a light on one side of the camera casts strong shadows that make the pattern stand out.

Special lights

Other evidence only shows up with special lighting. Ultraviolet radiation can make fingerprints, sweat, and urine glow. Scrubbed-away bloodstains also glow under purple light if they are sprayed with a special chemical (see page 20).

Telltale marks

A trail of blood, a cluster of bullet holes, or a series of scratches on a window ledge—all of these marks at a crime scene have a story to tell. They are all forms of pattern evidence. Reading and understanding them helps detectives reconstruct a crime. The shape of the marks and their position can show the way that a criminal broke into a house, where a killer was standing—and even whether they were right- or left-handed!

▲ Patterns of blood tell a story of violent crime. The shape and size of the blood spots show how far the blood flew or fell, as well as the direction in which it was traveling. Blood pools on the ground tell detectives where a victim lay injured or dying. These patterns are numbered to help detectives describe the crime scene.

Putting marks together

Individual marks in pattern evidence may not be important by themselves—for example, a single groove in a window frame might tell investigators very little. But taken together, all of the marks that make up the pattern say a lot more. These scratches and indentations are called tool marks. For example, marks made by a tool when forcing open a door can be matched back to the tool.

Unique marks

Sometimes tool marks only show what type of tool the criminal used. However, worn tools have scratches and marks that make them unique. When an old crowbar is used to open a window, the tool presses a pattern into the paint that is as unique as a signature. If police find the crowbar, they can compare its marks with the pattern evidence and accuse its owner.

Arms and ammunition

Guns also tell a story—or even two since there are two parts to every bullet. The lead slug fired from the barrel marks or pierces everything that it strikes. This pattern shows detectives how the bullet flew. The other part of the bullet, the cartridge case, does not fly down the barrel. Instead it is usually ejected to one side. So the pattern of cases can show where an assassin was standing in order to shoot.

◄ The pattern of cracks in shattered windows does not only show where the bullets flew. It also shows the order in which they were fired. The cracks from each bullet will not cross a crack caused by a bullet fired earlier.

▶ Careful burglars wear gloves to avoid leaving fingerprints, but the tools that they use to force their way in may also leave a pattern that can lead detectives to them.

Charting patterns

Investigators at the crime scene use measurements and cameras to gather and preserve pattern evidence. For example, where a shooting has taken place detectives mark the position of the ejected cartridge cases with numbered tabs and photograph them before collecting them for analysis (see page 54). In order to document a bullet's flight, they retrace it using cords, rods, or laser beams.

Analyzing blood marks is a special skill. Detectives chart the angles of splattered drops using marked lines, threads, or a computer. The drops point to where the victim was standing when they were wounded.

Guns, blood, and tools are not the only things that leave telltale patterns. Broken glass, burns, and furniture may leave marks that an alert detective can use to solve a crime.

◀ Laser beams are a convenient way to follow the path of a bullet from the gun barrel to the victim, but they do not show up on regular photographs. Filling the scene with smoke reveals the laser beam as a vivid, colored line and may show the likely direction for the recovery of the bullet if it missed its intended victim.

Finding a body

Suspicious deaths are a special challenge for investigators. Since murder is the most serious crime, they need to be extraordinarily careful about preserving any evidence that they might find on or around the body. Even the temperature of the body itself is important because it can show when the victim died. However, the first step is to make sure that the "corpse" is actually dead, so investigators always check for signs of life—even if this means destroying clues.

Looking for signs of life

Investigators look for breathing and a pulse. If the victim shows these "vital signs," investigators call an ambulance and start first aid.

If there are no signs of life, there is little that investigators can do except await the arrival of a forensic pathologist and a photographer. Pathologists are medical doctors who study diseases and injuries and their causes. Forensic pathologists specialize in the harm that crime does to the human body.

◄ Throughout the examination the forensic photographer is at the pathologist's elbow. These two work as a team to record the death scene as precisely as possible. Together, their notes and pictures form an important link in the chain of evidence that they hope will convict the killer.

Time of death

Before the pathologist touches the corpse, the photographer takes several pictures of it. This is necessary because the pathologist's examination will alter the crime scene and may change some of the evidence.

To determine when a person died, the pathologist takes the body's core temperature and that of the air. When the air is at 70°F (21°C), bodies cool by around 5°F (10°C) in 12 hours, so these two measurements show the time of death.

▶ Although the skin of a corpse feels cold, the body's core cools more slowly than the outside. In this picture, taken with a camera that records temperature differences using color, you can see that the warmest regions, tinted purple, are in the middle of the body.

Deadly stiffness

Next the pathologist checks for rigor mortis (death stiffness), which makes limbs difficult to move. It starts in the face and then spreads to the entire body in six to 12 hours. How far it has spread can indicate the time of death.

The pathologist also conducts a brief general examination of the body, looking only for evidence that may decay or disappear. Samples are taken from the mouth and the body's other openings. Some fluids may already have drained out; samples from the soil, floor, or furniture on which the victim lies confirm this.

Telltale tint

The pathologist also looks for red coloring. After death blood drains to the lower half of the body, giving it a pinker color. If this is anywhere else, the corpse may have been moved.

Finally, the body is taken to the laboratory. Within the body bag an extra layer of wrapping is placed on the head, hands, and feet. This makes it easier to identify and collect evidence that falls from these body parts.

▲ In hunts for missing people and victims of violent crimes police use specially trained tracker dogs as early in the investigation as they can. As the investigation expands, large numbers of searchers—often both police and volunteers—get involved. Their scents spread across the search area, which confuses the dogs.

Lifting prints

One very special type of pattern evidence has unique value to investigators. Fingerprints are the most personal of all patterns, and we leave them on almost everything we touch. They are formed by the whirling ridges on the skin of our hands. Everyone has a different pattern of ridges. The fingerprints that criminals leave behind can prove where they have been, what they have done—and, most important of all, who they are.

▲ A roll of tape is all it takes to lift prints from shiny objects at a crime scene. The glue holds prints firmly onto an evidence card.

The personal touch

Investigators look very carefully for fingerprints. Sometimes they are obvious, but more often criminals do not make the detectives' work easy. The prints that clean hands leave behind, even on glossy surfaces such as glass or metal, are hard to see unless the light shines from exactly the right angle. On rougher and patterned surfaces, such as paper, fingerprints may be completely invisible.

Latent prints

In order to find these hidden or "latent" prints on glossy surfaces, officers use dusting brushes to coat the surfaces that criminals may have touched with fine powder. The powder sticks to traces of grease and sweat that mark the fingerprints. To avoid smudging prints on very shiny surfaces, officers use powder mixed with iron dust, applying it with a magnetic brush that does not touch the surface.

Recording the marks

The next step is to preserve the prints so that they can be used as evidence. First officers take photographs of the prints. Then, if the object is small enough, they move it to the crime lab, being careful not to disturb the prints. If the prints are on an object that cannot be moved, they lift them with special tape. By sticking the tape onto an evidence card, officers are able to file it and find it again.

◀ Detectives who are looking for fingerprint evidence start in the obvious places. At home nobody wears gloves to type, so this officer is dusting a computer keyboard.

Casting deep prints

Fingerprints are not the only prints that investigators study at crime scenes. They also look for the prints left by bare feet and shoes—as well as for the tracks of vehicle tires.

Officers at the crime scene record deeply pressed footprints, shoe prints, ear prints, and tire tracks, first with a camera and then by pouring a liquid casting compound into the hollow shape left by the print. This sets into a solid lump within minutes, creating a permanent record that detectives can match with the feet, shoes, or vehicle of a suspect.

Footprints and shoe prints left on a carpet or floor are more difficult to record. Often if the prints are hard

▲ Tire tracks at an accident enable investigators to reconstruct what happened. They can show how fast each vehicle was moving, which way each driver was turning the steering wheel, and when they stepped on the brakes.

to photograph, officers try to lift them. To do this, several different devices can be used. On hard floors gel is used—a sheet of sticky material that picks up the pattern in the dust or dirt. If there are prints left on documents or paper, officers use an electrostatic lifter. This is a foil sheet that is coated in black plastic and connected to a device that generates a high-static electrical charge. The static charge pulls the dust from the print onto the plastic, where it can be seen more easily.

▼ Shoe prints from sneakers are valuable evidence because no two styles have the same tread pattern. Matching style alone is not enough to prove that a suspect's shoes left prints at a crime scene—wear marks and cuts in the soles must also match.

Showing the invisible

At the scene of a bloody murder the killer painstakingly cleans up. Buckets of detergent erase all the stains of the horrible crime that happened there . . . or do they? When investigators arrive, they are suspicious. They spray the crime scene with special chemicals—and a pattern of glowing bloodstains appears on the walls and floor. It sounds like magic, but it is pure forensic science. Detectives have a large and growing toolbox of chemicals and methods that make hidden clues visible.

Searching for blood

Signs of crimes are not always easy to see. Investigators have to work hard to find the clues that they need to catch criminals and prove their guilt.

Detectives need to know whether there is any blood at a crime scene and where it is. To find out, they spray any suspicious areas with chemicals such as luminol or fluorescein. These two chemicals make bloodstains glow in the dark, and even after scrubbing, there is still enough blood left to make the chemicals react. Although luminol glows for only a few seconds after spraying, fluorescein produces a longer-lasting glow when the stains are lit with a beam of ultraviolet light.

Revealing fingerprints

Just as these chemicals can reveal faint bloodstains, others can show weak prints on surfaces that are difficult or impossible to dust.

One of the best ways to make prints easier to see is to use cyanocrylate adhesive (superglue). This gives off a vapor that sticks to sweat in fingerprints and coats each line of the print with a hard, white plastic layer that shows up clearly. Detectives fumigate surfaces that might have fingerprints with superglue fumes or take small objects to the crime lab to process them in a fume-filled box.

◄ When used with dusts and dyes, laser light makes otherwise invisible prints show up clearly. Detectives wear colored goggles to protect their eyes and to make the prints appear clearer.

Problem prints

Wet or absorbent surfaces need different treatments. Ninhydrin, which is used on surfaces such as wallpaper, turns the sweat in fingerprints purple. DFO works in a similar way. It is 100 times more sensitive, but it needs an ultraviolet light to show the prints.

The case of Richard Rogers

Plastic bags dumped beside roads in New England in the 1990s hid grisly secrets—five men's bodies cut into pieces. Police were baffled for almost ten years until forensic scientists found a new way to make invisible fingerprints appear on plastic. Vacuum metal deposition (VMD) used gold vapor to reveal prints as clearly as a photograph. Comparing fingerprints from the bags with records from every U.S. state led detectives to New York nurse Richard Rogers. Gloves found with one body had been bought near his home. Rogers was arrested in 2001.

◀ The difference that fingerprint enhancement techniques make is obvious in this two-part picture. The right-hand side shows the faint print before it was sprayed with special chemicals. The left-hand side shows how clearly every ridge can be seen after being treated with chemicals.

▶ The bright glow from enhanced fingerprints is called fluorescence. Fluorescent substances like this laboratory chemical absorb invisible radiation and convert its energy into colored light that we can see and photograph.

SUMMARY OF CHAPTER 1: SIGNS OF THE CRIME

Clues at the scene

Investigators search the crime scene for evidence that might lead them to the person who committed the crime. If they cannot collect evidence immediately, they protect it until it can be safely recorded. They also take care of any victims and interview witnesses. Crime scene officers make notes, measure, and take pictures of any evidence. Crime scene photographers use special lighting techniques to photograph faint details. They may use digital cameras so that they can see the results immediately.

Patterns of evidence

Usually the patterns of evidence reveal more than individual pieces. For example, blood spots tell officers about the weapon used, and patterns from bullets show where a killer stood and how the bullets flew.

Fingerprints are a special type of pattern evidence. Everyone's fingertips are different, so their prints are a useful means of identification. However, fingerprints are not easy to see. Detectives make them clearer by dusting them with powder. Photographing the prints or lifting them with tape preserves them. Detectives also record footprints and tire tracks on soft ground by casting impressions. They lift dusty prints from documents with a special electrostatic mat. Investigators even have ways to find invisible marks. They use chemical sprays and UV lights to make scrubbed-away blood show up.

Corpses

The most grisly discovery at a crime scene is a dead body. A pathologist checks the body's temperature and stiffness in order to judge its time of death. Red marks show whether the body was moved, and samples of body fluids are taken too, before the body is sent to the laboratory.

Go further . . .

To find out more about the various disciplines of forensic science—and to play a detective game—visit:
www.library.thinkquest.org/17049/gather/index.en.shtml

Find the clues and solve the mystery of the barefoot burglar at:
www.cyberbee.com/whodunnit/crimescene.html

Take a virtual field trip and find out more about the FBI and how they solve crimes:
www.fbi.gov/kids/k5th/kidsk5th.htm

Eyewitness: Crime & Detection by Brian Lane (DK Children, 1998)

Crime scene manager
Controls the crime scene, supervises crime scene officers, gives information to news media, and communicates with police headquarters.

Crime scene officer
Protects the crime scene, collects and preserves evidence, takes fingerprints, and documents the scene.

Evidence assistant
Receives, tracks, and catalogs evidence from the crime scene and makes sure that it is available at a trial.

Forensic imaging specialist
Handles photography and videotaping at the crime scene, often using special lighting techniques.

Visit the New York City Police Museum:
100 Old Slip
New York, NY 10005
Phone: (212) 480-3100
www.nycpolicemuseum.org

Travel through 300 years of crime and punishment, reliving the lives, trials, and executions of some of Nottingham, England's, most notorious criminals. Crack the case and use forensics to help solve the crimes: Nottingham Galleries of Justice Nottingham, England NG1 1HN
Phone: +44 115 952 0555
www.galleriesofjustice.org.uk

14:53:06

14:53:47

14:54:18

14:54:57

CCTV images show a car thief in action

CHAPTER 2

Who is it?

Y ou are unique. This is not a compliment; it's a simple fact. Each human is different from every other one.

However, knowing that everyone is different is not the same as showing it. When detectives want to identify a criminal or a victim, they have to find all the things about a person that make him or her different from others.

The surest way to do this is with DNA analysis: a study of the human body's biological "master plan." However, this is slow and expensive. Comparing a face to a photograph is possibly the easiest way, but it is surprisingly unreliable. Fingerprints are such a sensitive test of identity that they can even prove that identical twins are different people.

Evidence from blood

Pumping through our veins or collecting in a vivid, red pool, blood can show detectives exactly who we are— or who we used to be when we were alive. Blood and other body fluids, such as saliva, are so important to forensic science that their study has its own name: serology. Serologists have developed a wide range of identity tests. DNA testing is the newest, but other tests have been around for 100 years.

Different types of blood

Blood is our life fluid—if we lose too much, we could die. Doctors have known this for hundreds of years, but when they tried to "top up" lost blood with blood given by a healthy person, their patients often died. Biologist Karl Landsteiner (1868–1943) discovered why. He showed that people have different blood types. Most of us have one of four types, which he called types A, B, AB, and O.

Blood tests

In 1902 Landsteiner helped devise a "blood typing" test for bloodstains. The test showed the group to which a stain belonged, so he suggested that detectives could use the test to solve crimes. For example, they could test bloodstains found on a murder suspect's clothes and compare them to the blood of the victim. Matching the two blood types could help prove the suspect's guilt.

However, because out of every ten people, roughly four have type A blood and five have type O, the test was not a very accurate way of proving a suspect's guilt. But it was much better at proving innocence. If the bloodstained clothes did not match the victim's blood, police could be sure that the suspect did not commit the crime. Today, when investigators find blood at a crime scene, they still use the "ABO blood test" to eliminate suspects. However, before they do this they carry out even simpler tests.

◀ The "ABO blood test" uses two test solutions called antibodies. "Anti-A" solution makes type A blood cells form clumps. Type B blood clumps with "Anti-B." Type AB blood clumps with both, and type O does not clump with either one.

▼ Our bodies contain 5–6 L (10pt) of blood. But in order to identify a suspect, serologists only need one forty-millionth of a drop (shown here greatly magnified).

▶ To analyze blood, technicians first use clean, sterilized instruments to carefully remove the stain. Then they moisten it with saltwater in order to turn it into a liquid sample for testing.

Is it really blood?
The first of these tests is what forensic detectives call a presumptive test for blood. It shows whether or not it is safe to presume that a stain really is blood. This is not as silly as it sounds: blood is not always easy to recognize, and it is easy to confuse with other substances.

Spraying for evidence
The luminol and fluorescein sprays (see page 20) that detectives use to see bloodstains are presumptive tests themselves, but there are many other tests that can be used. The easiest to use are Hemastix—small tabs with a test chemical on one end. Investigators at the crime scene moisten a stick and rub it on the stain. If it is blood, the tip of the Hemastix turns from yellow to green.

Blood or sauce?
Although these tests are very helpful for detectives who are looking for blood at a crime scene, they do not provide all the answers. Horseradish, for example, contains chemicals that are similar to blood, so a stain that passes a presumptive test for blood may in fact turn out to be the remains of someone's dinner.

▶ Technicians in a serology laboratory prepare samples for testing. One of the first checks is to determine if the blood is human. Serologists use the precipitin test for this. Dropped into a test tube or forced across a piece of sticky gel by an electric current, the sample forms a clear line where it meets the test chemical.

DNA analysis

The police charge a shoplifter and take a sample on a swab from the inside of his mouth in order to analyze his DNA. Although the thief has not been arrested before, they find that the swab matches the DNA from the scene of a brutal, unsolved murder committed many years earlier. When they question the thief, he breaks down and admits to the killing. It sounds like a detective's dream, but it is happening now. Invented in 1984, DNA analysis has become an important weapon in the fight against crime.

▲ Identical twins do not just look similar. They really are exactly the same—down to the last gene. DNA analysis cannot tell them apart but can easily distinguish between ordinary siblings.

Genes and DNA

Within the cells of our bodies there is a tiny strand of protein called DNA—deoxyribonucleic acid. Half of our DNA, called genes, comes from each of our parents—this is why we look like them.

Genes only make up part of our DNA—the rest consists of regular patterns of proteins. These also come from our parents, but the number of times they are repeated is unique to each person. Because our DNA is unique—but similar to our relatives—it is a useful method of identifying people.

Extracting DNA

If investigators at a crime scene find a drop of blood or saliva, the crime lab can extract DNA from it. Comparing the extracted DNA with the suspect's DNA can confirm whether or not they were involved in the crime—or even whether the suspect's mother or son was involved.

In order to make the comparison, the lab first extracts DNA and mixes it with special chemicals that multiply the repeated patterns until there is enough material to test.

Racing for a result

Next the technicians mark each repeated pattern with a dye and "race" the strands down a narrow tube. A sensor at the tube's end identifies each colored strand and feeds the data into a computer. The results form a DNA profile, or "fingerprint," that identifies who the sample came from.

The final step is to compare the results to a suspect's DNA sample. If there is no suspect, detectives look for a match in a computer file listing the DNA profiles of known criminals.

◀ At a crime scene investigators collect biological samples using cotton swabs. Stored in a perfectly clean tube and often containing a preservative, the swab is chilled to make sure that the DNA in the sample does not decay before it is analyzed.

Identifying the dead

When a tsunami ripped across the Indian Ocean on December 26, 2004, thousands of people died. Towering waves tore away clothes and possessions that might have shown who the victims were. Within a few days the corpses were so swollen because of the tropical heat that even close family members could not recognize them. Governments turned to DNA testing to identify the dead. They took samples from victims' bodies and from survivors who had lost relatives. Matching the DNA profiles allowed families to bury lost parents or children.

Perfect proof?

Investigators use DNA not only to match suspects to crimes but also to identify bodies that are beyond recognition. DNA is also sensitive—just one forty-millionth of a drop of blood can produce a result.

However, DNA tests are not foolproof. Samples can be polluted with DNA from other sources, confusing the results. On small islands where everyone is related the DNA is very similar, and DNA profiling is not a very reliable way of proving guilt.

▶ Working with tiny samples of bodily fluids, serologists mix DNA from a suspect or crime scene with a chemical "amplifier." In a process called polymerase chain reaction (PCR) the chemical increases the amount of DNA in the sample until there is enough to test.

Teeth and bones

How do you identify a bag of bones? Skulls and skeletons are often all that is left of the victims of crimes once fire or animals have consumed the flesh. Figuring out who was burned or buried is the job of forensic anthropologists. Using teeth and bones as clues, they can estimate the victim's sex, age, height, and race. Forensic dentists can even give a skull a name if they can compare the teeth to dental records.

▼ The casts that dentists take when fitting dentures give forensic anthropologists an ideal way of identifying rotted or burned bodies. Most often they use dental records or X-rays or—where these do not exist—descriptions from friends and family.

▼ By assembling a skeleton, scientists can estimate how tall a crime victim was when they were alive. Where some bones are missing, the most reliable guide to height is the femur (thighbone). Our height is around 3 ¾ times the length of this bone.

▶ At the scene of a major fire or other disaster forensic dentists use portable X-ray machines to record the teeth of the bodies. The X-rays reveal gaps (dark patches) and fillings (light patches). Matching the patterns to dental records helps identify victims.

Bleached or blackened bones

Human bodies do not last long. In warm weather it only takes animals and bacteria one month to pick every scrap of flesh off a corpse left out in the open air. Fire is an even quicker way to blot out identity—an intense fire can reduce a body to bones in one hour or less.

To the untrained eye skeletons are little more than grisly signs of death. However, to a forensic anthropologist they are like an open book, filled with information about the living.

Young or old?

To estimate age, anthropologists look at the growth of teeth and bones. Children's first teeth appear at around six months of age. These grow and change continuously until the last permanent teeth grow in at around the age of 13.

For teenagers and adults bone growth is a better guide to age. At birth bones are soft and separate; they grow harder and fuse (join) together in a set order. The long bones, for example, have separate ends until around the age of 13, when they fuse together. The clavicle (collarbone) is the last bone to fuse, when a person is around 28 years old. For older people forensic anthropologists also look at the shape of the ends of the ribs. These become more hollow and spikier as age increases. Wear and tear on the joints and teeth is also a good guide to a skeleton's age.

▶ A woman's pelvis (hip bones) must be wide enough for a baby's head to pass through during childbirth. Men have much narrower hips, and the difference in the size of these bones makes them the easiest way to judge the sex of a skeleton.

Female pelvis

Male pelvis

Marks on the skeleton

Skilled anthropologists can read even more from a skeleton. From the points where muscle meets bone they can judge how strong the person was. Distinctive patterns of wear may give hints about the type of work they did. Injuries and a few diseases also leave recognizable marks on the skeleton.

Man or woman?

Looking at the shape of bones, rather than their size, reveals the sex of the victim. The pelvis (hip bones) shows this most clearly since women have much wider hips than men.

Looking at the skull

There are less obvious clues to be found on the skull. For example, the skull's shape can hint at the race or ethnic background of the dead person. White people have round skulls, with jaws directly below their eyebrows. People with African ancestors have more oval skulls and faces that slope back from the jaw to the eyes.

Open wide!

Teeth are the last parts to rot or burn, so a skull—or just one jaw—may be enough to identify a body. Dentists look for filled, bridged, capped, or missing teeth and compare them to dental charts or X-rays. This method of identification is especially valuable in fires or transportation disasters, where anthropologists try to match scorched bodies to a list of known victims.

▼ Measuring the skull can help an anthropologist tell whether a victim was black, white, or Asian. The height of the skull is also important. Added to the length of the back, hip, leg, and foot bones, it shows how tall the dead person was.

KNOX TRAIL LIBRARY

Making faces

Without flesh, eyes, or hair, a skull cannot give any clues about the appearance, personality, and character of the face that once smiled from it. But the bones of the skull are the foundations of the face. By building on them with clay or software, forensic sculptors and computer artists can reconstruct the faces of the dead. Their lifelike images may enable witnesses to identify a murder victim.

Reconstruction starts

Attempts to recreate faces from skulls of the dead started in Germany in the 1880s. Anatomists (scientists who study the human body) used needles and knives to measure the depth of flesh on the faces of corpses. With this knowledge, they were able to mold the right thickness of clay onto casts of the skulls in order to create a likeness. This method of reconstruction continued unchanged for more than 100 years, until computer technology made it possible to recreate faces more precisely.

Three-dimensional scanning

Using a three-dimensional (3-D) scanner, the position and shape of every bone can be recorded. The result is a 3-D model that can be viewed from any angle.

Today information about the thickness of muscle, fat, and skin on the face now comes from living subjects instead of from corpses. Computer tomography (CT) scans create 3-D images of both bone and soft tissue such as muscle. This makes it possible to measure flesh depths without using needles or knives. Not only is this safe and painless, but it also gives more accurate results than measuring corpses. After death muscles relax, and the face sags.

Merge and match

Technicians merge the scan of an unidentified skull with the CT scan of a person of the same age, sex, and race. Then they "warp" the skull of the CT scan, stretching or squashing it until the two virtual skulls are the same size. Warping the CT skull also creates an accurate simulation of the flesh layers on the dead person's skull.

◄ Computer modeling applies layers of virtual "flesh" onto a scan of a skull. Once the model is complete, it is easy to make the face look fatter or thinner and older or younger.

▲ Just as a facial reconstruction builds faces from the skulls of the dead, composite photos can create a likeness of the living. By making a "jigsaw puzzle" out of a library of face parts, witnesses build up pictures of suspects or missing people.

◀ Rebuilding faces from skulls is based on science and years of experience. The bones of the face do not provide clues as to the shape of the lips, ears, eyes, and nose, so forensic artists must guess what the features looked like.

▲ To reconstruct a face, X-ray photographs are taken of the skull, and a replica is made to show the shape.

▲ Pins are placed at key points where muscles attach.

▲ Muscles are then added in the right places on the skull.

▲ Finally, the cartilage, skin, and eyes are added.

The result is a virtual view of the face as if created from white clay. Technicians then add color and texture using a "color map." This is a photograph of someone whom investigators believe resembles their subject. Like the CT scan, the texture wraps around the surface of the model.

▶ After building a face, technicians make a plaster cast from the clay model. Plaster is white, so to make it look more lifelike, skilled artists carefully paint the surface of the clay.

Finishing touches

The computer then calculates the appearance of every point on the face, building a view from one angle or from many. This gives either an ordinary portrait with photographic realism or a virtual head that witnesses or relatives can view on-screen from any angle.

▲ When making computerized reconstructions of faces, technicians can add glasses, hair, beards, and mustaches from a list. Without these clues, it is often difficult to recognize even the faces of relatives or close friends.

Matching fingerprints

A record of every criminal's fingerprints seems like a great way to identify suspects. However, a fingerprint collection is useless unless detectives can search it easily for fingerprints that match those they find at the crime scene. Detectives found a way of doing this more than 100 ago. Today computer databases take seconds to compare a crime scene print against millions of criminal records.

Fingerprint breakthrough

When a hospital in Tokyo, Japan, was burglarized in 1879, the police were sure that they knew who was responsible. But the man they accused was saved from punishment by a friend, Henry Faulds (1843–1930). Visiting the crime scene, Faulds spotted a dirty fingerprint that the burglar had left on a wall. He pointed out that none of the patterns on his friend's fingertips matched the thief's print. It was the first time that fingerprints had been used in a criminal case.

▼ Fingerprint classification systems plot where ridges end or fork (shown here as round blobs). Fingerprint examiners would be confident that they had identified a suspect if a dozen of these "minutiae" from the criminal's record matched a print from the crime scene.

▼ Detectives scan the prints they find, and the Integrated Automatic Fingerprint Identification Systems (IAFIS) computer tries to match them with those of known criminals' prints. The system presents the closest matches on-screen so that detectives can compare them with those of the suspect.

▶ Traditional police files record suspects' fingerprints by pressing or rolling the inked fingertips onto one card each. To make searching possible, fingerprint examiners split up these ten prints and classify each one individually.

Computer searches

Today computer systems do a lot of the searching. Detectives scan the hands of convicted criminals, and for each fingertip computers analyze and encode the "minutiae." These are the distinctive features such as the points where ridges branch, fork, or end.

When detectives find a print at a crime scene, they scan it, and the computer tries to match its minutiae with the prints on file. The closest matches are presented for detectives to make the final comparison.

Integrated Automatic Fingerprint Identification Systems (IAFIS) can search one million fingerprint records in less than one second. The system in use in the U.S. contains more than 40 million prints, and 700 are added each day.

Classifying fingerprints

To make searching practical, detectives divide the prints according to their basic shapes: loops, arches, and whorls (see left). Then each group is split according to the number of ridges, their direction, and other details.

Classifying the fingerprints in this way means that the number of possible matches could be reduced from thousands to dozens. Searching the prints becomes more practical—just as the alphabetical arrangement of a dictionary helps you find a word quickly.

Ramirez is caught!

In 1985 the people of Los Angeles, California, were terrified when a serial killer prowled their city. In August a man he had shot survived and described the killer's car. Police found it and checked for fingerprints. They only found one, but by using the city's IAFIS, they matched it to Richard Ramirez. His picture was flashed on TV, and he was arrested the next day. At his 1988 trial Ramirez was found guilty of 13 murders and sentenced to death.

▶ By storing fingerprints as digital records, like this one from the French police service, fingerprint examiners can search one million records in less than one second.

Unknown culprit

When there is no obvious suspect for a crime, detectives start eliminating people from their inquiries. By ruling out everyone who seems unlikely to have committed the crime, they narrow down their investigation to the few people who might possibly be guilty. When even this approach fails, they may turn to offender profiling—a method of identifying criminals by studying how they commit their crimes.

▶ In the incident room at a police station officers plot sightings of a suspect on a wall map. Phone calls and sightings of cars are all recorded to build up a picture of where the suspect has been. This helps them narrow down their search area.

◀ When criminals run from a crime scene, witnesses may not see enough of them to provide a full description. Nevertheless, the smallest details about weight, age, and fitness can help police piece together a profile of their suspect.

Catching a killer

A woman is gunned down on a busy city street. Witnesses who heard the shots saw a young man quickly run away from the scene. He dived into a car and drove away at high speed. Evidence at the crime scene tells detectives very little, so how do they find the killer?

When the investigation begins, everyone is a potential suspect. The police need to eliminate entire groups of people in order to narrow down their search. They start with the sex of the attacker. Half of the population is female, so already they have reduced the number of suspects by 50 percent. Because the killer was a young man, the police can rule out anyone under the age of 16 or over 40. He sprinted from the scene—so the suspect is reasonably physically fit. Detectives may also eliminate people who cannot drive since he escaped in a car.

Offender profiles

Forensic scientists have tried to improve on this traditional approach by looking at what type of people commit crimes. From the few clues they have they try to build a profile (a shape or pattern) of what the criminal was probably like.

Catching the New York bomber

One of the first profiling cases led to the arrest of New York's "Mad Bomber," who planted 30 bombs in the city over 16 years. In 1957, when conventional attempts to catch the bomber failed, detectives turned to psychiatrist Dr. James Brussel.

Brussel told them that the bomber was a man, as female criminals rarely use bombs. He sent bombs and threats to Con. Edison—the city's electric company—so possibly he was fired by the company or hated it for some other reason. His handiwork on the bombs showed that he was neat and precise. The formal language of his letters suggested that he was foreign and was probably east European because people from this region had used bombs in the past. Dr. Brussel even predicted that when he was arrested, the bomber would be wearing an old-fashioned suit, buttoned up.

From this, a secretary at Con. Edison found the records of a man who had been injured there years before. He fit the doctor's description perfectly, and when police swooped in on his home, they found him wearing his suit, buttoned up!

▶ Identifying a suspect is usually a process of elimination. Gender, age, physical fitness, and abilities can all help the police pinpoint a criminal within a social group. By eliminating large sections of the population from their inquiries, the police are able to focus their resources on the remaining section and find their suspect.

▶ House-to-house inquiries, like this one in France, help the police identify criminals. The police ask standard questions to each resident in order to build up a picture of the local community and find out if their suspect is known there.

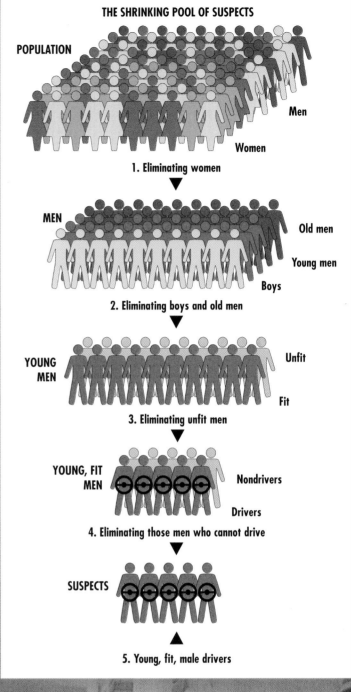

THE SHRINKING POOL OF SUSPECTS

POPULATION

Men

Women

1. Eliminating women

MEN

Old men

Young men

Boys

2. Eliminating boys and old men

YOUNG MEN

Unfit

Fit

3. Eliminating unfit men

YOUNG, FIT MEN

Nondrivers

Drivers

4. Eliminating those men who cannot drive

SUSPECTS

5. Young, fit, male drivers

Proof of guilt

"He's the man. I am sure. I saw him with my own eyes." Witness statements like these can persuade us of a suspect's guilt, but can we really trust them? Research shows that witnesses find it difficult to pick out criminals from lineups and albums of mug shots. Blurry security camera pictures make it even harder. Other modern crime-fighting aids, such as lie detectors, seem like equally unreliable witnesses.

Never forget a face

We all trust our memories, especially when we think back to an experience as dramatic as a crime. However, identifying someone we have only seen for a moment—possibly weeks earlier—is more difficult than it seems.

In a lineup a suspect stands in a row of similar-looking people. Out of their sight an officer asks the witness to point out who they saw. Some are able to choose correctly, but wrong identification is common.

Facing up to the truth

Mug shot albums do not have a much better track record. Witnesses are asked to look at photographs of previously convicted criminals who match the description that has been given to the police. The person that the witness picks out may then become a suspect—even if there is no other evidence against them.

▶ CCTV cameras can record city dwellers during their everyday activities. They can show the police if a suspect was in the area when a crime was committed.

◀ The film from closed-circuit television (CCTV) is commonly used as evidence for the police. It can show them if a person matching the suspect's description was involved in the crime.

Composite faces

The police also use composite photos, or "photo fit." A witness describes who they saw commit the crime, and an officer puts together a picture of the suspect's face from a variety of photographs of mouths, eyes, ears, chins, noses, and hairstyles. Police officers then use this picture to search for a suspect. Newspapers often publish the composites to encourage members of the public to join in the search.

► The polygraph, or lie detector, monitors changes in a suspect's sweating, heartbeat, and breathing. These changes may indicate that they are lying. However, tests have shown that clever criminals can beat the lie detector.

Protecting the innocent

Despite their problems, all of these methods and machines, such as closed-circuit television (CCTV), can help catch criminals. Used wisely and fairly, police officers can imprison those who are actually guilty. To take full advantage of them, detectives first must realize that memory is unreliable. To protect innocent people, they must look at the whole picture and not rely on identification alone.

SUMMARY OF CHAPTER 2: WHO IS IT?

Identifying the criminal and the victim

A lot of an investigator's work is concerned with identity. Who committed the crime? Whose body has been found?

An "ABO blood test" can help find an answer. It shows to which of four groups someone's blood belongs. If blood at a crime scene is not in the same group as a suspect's blood, then police know that they have arrested the wrong person.

DNA testing is an accurate way to check identity. Forensic scientists extract DNA from blood or tissue samples. Testing produces a string of numbers that is unique to that person. Matching numbers from a crime scene sample and a suspect greatly increases the possibility that the suspect committed the crime.

Some other trusted methods of identifying people are surprisingly unreliable—witnesses make mistakes when they look for suspects' faces in mug shots or lineups.

Crimes with no suspect

When there are no witnesses, no blood samples, and no photographs for detectives to work with, identifying a suspect is especially difficult. Investigators start by eliminating everyone who could not possibly have been at the scene. Occasionally they try offender profiling, using what they know about the crime to guess what type of person did it.

Fingerprints also lead detectives to an unknown suspect. If detectives find prints at the crime scene, they search their files of previous offenders to find a match. As these files grew, searches took longer, but today computers speed up the process.

Investigators cannot use fingerprints to identify long-dead or burned victims. Instead they look at the size and shape of bones and teeth. These are clues to age, weight, sex, and race. Teeth can tell detectives exactly who they have found—but only if they have dental records. If these are not available, forensic anthropologists use crime victims' skulls to recreate their faces. With clay or computer software, they build up a likeness—although they have to guess the look of the ears, eyes, lips, and nose.

Go further . . .

 Find out about the history of fingerprinting and how it helps solve crimes at: www.cyberbee.com/ whodunnit/fp.html

Discover basic information about the structure and function of DNA as it relates to DNA fingerprinting at: www.protist.biology.washington. edu/fingerprint/dnaintro.html

Use math and forensic science to figure out the relationship between the length of your foot and your height at: www.cyberbee.com/ whodunnit/foot.html

KFK Genes & DNA by Richard Walker (Kingfisher, 2003)

 Forensic anthropologist
Studies human remains to estimate the age, sex, height, and other facts, as well as to help identify the body.

Forensic entomologist
Investigates insect activity connected to a crime and uses their knowledge of insect life cycles to find out the date and time of death.

Forensic pathologist
Studies the bodies of crime victims both inside and out. Also tries to figure out what killed them.

Forensic technician
Helps forensic scientists by preparing evidence, maintaining equipment, and recording results.

 Explore the police cells while discovering more about crime, forensic science, forgery, and international policing:
Greater Manchester Police Museum
Manchester, England M1 1ES
Phone: +44 0 161 856 3287
www.gmp.police.uk/
about_gmp/history.asp

Take a fascinating tour of the nation's first permanent genetics exhibition, *Genetics: Decoding Life*, at the Museum of Science and Industry.
Chicago Museum of Science and Industry
Chicago, IL 60637
Phone: (773) 684-1414
www.msichicago.org

Examining evidence in a laboratory

CHAPTER 3

Crime lab

Sometimes all it takes to solve a crime is a single strand of hair, a fleck of paint, or a drop of blood that is too small to see without a microscope.

Forensic scientists look for this and much more at a crime laboratory—a specialist center where technicians can analyze, study, and test the evidence found at crime scenes. In the smallest labs technicians might do all the work

But bigger laboratories have specialists who concentrate on just one field of forensic science.

Our tour of the crime laboratory starts in the autopsy room. This is where medical examiners, called pathologists, carry out detailed studies of the bodies of crime victims and people who die in suspicious ways. Not only can they determine how people died but also when they died.

The autopsy

With its white tiles, bright lights, and shiny benches, the autopsy room looks like an operating room. But instead of surgeons, forensic pathologists are the ones who wield the scalpels. During autopsies bodies are cut open in order to find out how a person died. An autopsy is the most detailed part of the postmortem (after death) investigation. This investigation is a thorough study that includes photographs and X-rays of the body, as well as a complete inspection of its appearance.

Starting on the outside

Because every suspicious death is different, no two autopsies are exactly alike. However, most autopsies begin with the careful removal of clothing from the body and their examination for evidence. The pathologist weighs the body and takes a close look at its outside appearance. Cuts, bruises, scars, and identifying marks must all be noted. These are dictated into a tape recorder.

The external examination and X-ray photographs guide pathologists when they begin to dissect (cut up) the body. If the cause of death is not obvious, it is common to do an autopsy of the entire body. By following standard procedures, pathologists investigate all of the organs of the body in order to establish the cause of death.

A general autopsy

The pathologist begins by opening up the body cavity using razor-sharp blades and saws or bone cutters. A slit, or a T- or Y-shaped cut up the front of the body, brings the internal organs within reach. The pathologist removes the organs, taking careful records of any injuries before weighing them individually. Taking samples of fluids and tissues from each organ makes it possible for toxicologists (see page 52) to test for the presence of drugs, poisons, or alcohol. The skull does not escape attention either—to study the brain it is necessary to cut around the bones of the head.

Looking for signs

Pathologists look for subtle signs that are easy to miss. For example, strangulation often causes no obvious injuries on the outside of the body—these telltale signs lie beneath the skin. To be certain that their subject was strangled, pathologists must drain all the blood from the neck and carefully peel back the layers of tissue. This reveals the tiny bruises that confirm the crime. Stabbing victims also need special attention in order to trace the path of the knife through the flesh.

Essential notes

The pathologists' investigation is useless unless they write down what they have found. Their autopsy reports can help expose murders that have been disguised as suicide, or they can free someone wrongly accused of killing by showing that the "victim" died of natural causes.

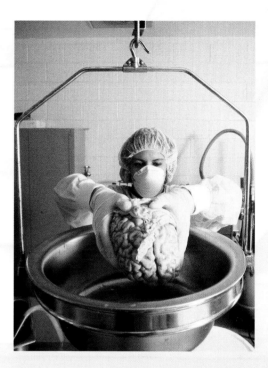

▲ Pathologists weigh body parts that they remove during an autopsy. Many diseases cause a change in weight of the body's organs, so this information must appear in the autopsy report.

◄ Pathologists do not work alone. An assistant from the morgue (body storage area) lifts the corpse onto a stainless steel table and helps with certain jobs, such as sawing open the skull, that do not need the pathologist's skill.

How did they die?

If only corpses could speak, they could tell investigators exactly how they died. Even autopsies cannot give these silent witnesses voices, but they can discover some of their secrets. From their bumps and bruises and cuts and burns, the forensic pathologist can often piece together the story of a crime victim's last moments. Along with evidence from the crime scene and statements from witnesses, the postmortem examination eliminates natural deaths from accidents, murders, and suicides.

The manner of death

Figuring out how someone died is important because it says whether or not a crime has been committed. If the death was natural or a suicide, the police may have nothing to investigate.

Pathologists call this important decision the "manner of death"— the way or method in which the victim died. They choose from four possibilities: natural death, accidental death, suicide, or homicide (deliberate killing).

The cause of death

Before making a choice the pathologist looks for the cause of death—what ended this person's life? Was it an injury such as a stab wound that caused massive bleeding? Perhaps electrocution stopped the heart. Or was it a fatal illness such as a sudden stroke? The answer may seem obvious, but pathologists have to consider every possible cause of death and decide which one is the most likely.

Suicide or murder?

For example, in the burned-out shell of a car police find the charred body of the owner. An empty gasoline can and a lighter in his hand tell the rest of the story. The pathologist's first step might be to look for soot in the lungs since people who are burned to death breathe in smoke. Clean lungs would suggest that the victim was dead before the fire was started and that he did not kill himself. Although burning a corpse destroys many clues, a closer examination might reveal the true cause of death. A skull fracture, for example, is all the proof that is needed to start a murder investigation.

The stealthy killer

Often the telltale signs of murder are not obvious at all. It is common for sick, frail, elderly people to die of natural causes, but pathologists study their dead faces very carefully. Slight bruising around the mouth and nose or pinprick-sized spots of blood beneath the skin on the neck suggest that they may have been smothered with a pillow. Such a discovery might send the police in search of a family member who could have gained by their elderly relative's death.

▼ By the time that the pathologist packs up her crime scene bag, she may already have suspicions about how the victim died. There may be further clues about this scattered around the crime scene, but collecting them is the job of crime scene officers. The pathologist's real work begins when she studies the body in the autopsy room. There she can look for internal evidence that even a fire could not destroy.

Sealing off the crime scene prevents curious onlookers from trampling on clues that might reveal the cause of death.

Careful handling of the corpse helps preserve evidence.

▲ A blow to the head does not always cause damage that is obvious, like the swelling on the right of this scan. Often a pathologist has to make a microscopic study of slices of the brain to spot the bleeding that caused death.

The pathologist examines the body's position and surroundings to help her understand how the victim died.

A crime scene officer's discovery of tire tracks suggests that the death might be suspicious, possibly because another vehicle left the crime scene.

Although firefighters may destroy evidence through their work, their first priority is to rescue anyone caught in the blaze.

Dust

Wool and synthetic fibers

Polyester fibers

Weave

Trace evidence

A brutal attacker, called "the Fox," scrapes his car at a crime scene. It leaves a fleck of paint 45 in. (115cm) up a tree. Microscopic studies show that the paint color is "harvest yellow." Thousands of cars are painted this color, but detectives track them all. One has a scratch 45 in. (115cm) from the ground. The owner confesses. These particles of paint, fibers, and glass, called trace evidence, link the car, the victim, and the crime scene in a chain of proof.

Swapping evidence

The attacks committed by "the Fox" in 1984 show the truth of an important idea—that every contact leaves a trace. Called "Locard's Exchange Principle," after the French detective who devised it, it is simple: at the scene of every crime there will be traces left behind by the criminal. Criminals also carry away traces that they picked up at the crime scene. In other words, there has been an exchange, or swapping, of trace evidence.

Collecting and studying traces

Trace evidence is often too tiny to see with the naked eye, so detectives collect it with tape or with a forensic vacuum cleaner. It is then studied under a microscope. There are five types of microscopes.

Ordinary microscopes light up trace evidence from behind, so they show clear details in only thin or transparent materials. Polarized light microscopes use filters to block out light. Many types of evidence, such as glass, "undo" the blocking, so they appear bright. Stereoscope microscopes have twin eyepieces and show the evidence in three dimensions. Comparison microscopes make it easy to study two similar pieces of evidence in order to see if they match. Electron microscopes reveal minute surface details on paint flakes, hair, and fibers.

◀ Whether it is found in dust or woven into fabric, the shape of a thread enables detectives to identify the fiber. However, fiber shape and color are only useful clues if they are unusual. White cotton, for example, is so common that it rarely helps link a suspect to a crime. These fibers are shown magnified thousands of times.

▶ A forensic vacuum cleaner sucks up trace evidence and collects it onto a paper filter. Magnifying the filter with a microscope shows the tiniest specks of dust.

How paint proves guilt

Putting a flake of paint under a microscope can show how many coats there are and the color of each one. Police can match car paints with makes, models, and years, as in the example of "the Fox." House paints can also offer useful clues. For example, if police find a flake of paint stuck to a suspect's crowbar, they might compare it with the paint on the window of a burglarized house. A match would suggest that the suspect was the burglar.

Looking closely at glass

Although one piece of glass looks a lot like another, a forensic laboratory can identify a tiny glass flake by measuring its light-bending power and its density (the weight of a standard piece). These tests could, for example, match a flake of glass found on a hit-and-run victim with the broken headlights on a car. If the pieces are large enough, fitting them together like a jigsaw puzzle would also prove the driver's guilt.

▶ When two vehicles collide, each one leaves traces of paint on the other. Here an investigator carefully pulls a paint flake loose from a crashed car. Its colors—and the order in which they were painted—will identify the make, model, and possibly even the age of the other car involved in the accident.

▼ To detectives, dirty fingernails do not mean bad hygiene—they are a vital source of trace evidence! When victims of violent crime struggle with their attackers, they may scratch off enough skin for DNA testing (see pages 26–27) to be done.

Fantastic fibers

Fibers from clothes look very different under a microscope. Natural fibers, such as wool, cotton, and linen, have distinctive shapes that make them easy to recognize. When they are dyed, their colors provide extra clues that help detectives find a match. For identifying artificial fibers, such as nylon, chemical tests are used.

Dirty proof

Mud, filth, dirt, dead insects—and live maggots. When cleaning the house, we sweep, scrub, and spray to get rid of these unwanted things, but forensic scientists actually collect them. Natural materials form a special type of trace evidence. Matching samples taken from the suspect, the victim, and the crime scene can prove a link between them—and living things, such as pollen, can also provide a calendar to show the season or time of a crime.

Mud as evidence

As criminals flee from a robbery, the wheels of their car spin in the dirt. When police find the car, they find mud in the wheel arches. Matching it to mud at the crime scene shows that the car was used in the robbery.

To confirm that two samples come from the same place, they are studied under a microscope, and the particle's size, shape, and type are compared. For example, land sand has sharp edges, but beach sand is rounded.

▲ With the aid of a stereoscopic microscope, forensic scientists can see tiny traces of dirt—even on apparently clean shoes taken from a suspect. The dirt will be evidence of guilt if it matches samples of soil at the crime scene.

▼ Forensic entomologists (insect experts) keep libraries of dead flies (top of the page) and their maggots (bottom). When they are found on corpses, a fly's stage of development allows detectives to estimate the time of death.

Picking flowers

Seeds and other parts of plants are used in a similar way. Microscopic examination helps identify what type of plant the material came from. Suspicions would increase if the seeds of an unusual plant found at the crime scene were found on a suspect's clothes.

Plants make pollen in the spring and seeds in the summer. So by studying dirty clothes, detectives might prove not only that a suspect visited a crime scene but also when they were there.

Hair samples

Like clothing fibers, hairs have special shapes and colors. These properties help forensic scientists match them—or at least guess where they are from. If you look at human hairs under a microscope, you will see some striking differences. Hairs from the scalp are round in cross section; those from the armpit are oval; and hairs from beards are roughly triangular. Hairs also store a record of lifestyle, pollution, and chemicals. For example, tests on the hairs can reveal if a suspect has a history of drug use.

The bugs that cleared a sailor

Soon after death flies may lay eggs on corpses, and the life cycle of the grubs that hatch show when the victims died.

A Hungarian ferry captain was accused of murder after a body was found on his ferry. An autopsy found fly eggs and grubs on the corpse. A forensic entomologist gave evidence that the eggs were from a type of fly that was only active during the day. The captain came on duty at 6 P.M., and the victim must have died earlier than this.

▼ Magnified many thousands of times, tiny pollen grains (colored purple here) from different plants look unique. Their shapes help detectives figure out what plants a suspect or victim might have touched.

Computers and crime

Today's wired world seems like the perfect playground for criminals. Corrupt programmers hack into banks' computer systems, steal money, and then vanish. However, escaping justice is becoming much harder as forensic science catches up with cyber crime. Computer experts know how to find clues hidden on hard drives and can track down those who use the Internet.

▲ Computer cheats can trick computer users into revealing their secret passwords. Spam e-mails ask victims to confirm their passwords by typing them in on bogus web sites that look identical to the official bank web site. Criminals then collect the passwords and steal the money.

More computers, more crimes

The spread of computers has made old crimes easier—for example, traditional blackmailers can now make their demands by e-mail. It has also led to new crimes. Computer viruses did not exist 25 years ago because too few people owned computers.

Computers become infected

Viruses are tiny programs that copy themselves. They are spread by e-mail and run invisibly, causing damage to computers. To find virus writers, computer security experts trace the spread of the "infection." They also look for clues in the virus code—often programmers hide their "signatures" in lines of code.

Melissa virus

In March 1999 millions of computer users opened "an important message" apparently from a trusted friend. In fact, it was a virus, and it caused more than $80 million worth of damage. The Internet service provider America Online (AOL) discovered that a subscriber had uploaded the virus, named Melissa, to one of its message boards. By looking at computer logs, AOL found the telephone number that the virus author used to dial in. This clue led the FBI to a New Jersey programmer, named David Smith, who was jailed for 20 months.

Computer fraud

Viruses that throttle the Internet make headlines, but forensic computer experts spend most of their time studying computers seized in crimes such as fraud. Recovering data from them is a difficult challenge, because

▼ Computer experts keep an eye out for hacker attacks by watching the flow of data and messages on the Internet. A sudden surge in volume may show that a new virus is spreading rapidly. Unless these "infections" are stopped, computers worldwide can choke on the junk messages that the virus creates.

even just turning on a computer can erase valuable evidence. So the technicians make an exact copy of the computer's hard drive without starting up the computer. By working on this copy, they leave the original untouched.

The way that computers store data makes the technicians' job easier. When criminals "erase" files from a hard drive, the data is not destroyed—the file just becomes invisible. Even criminals who completely wipe out letters and e-mails that might prove their guilt are not safe. Computers store multiple copies as temporary files. Electronic detectives can track down and read these duplicates.

Online fraud

In 1994 Vladimir Levin hacked into a Citibank computer in New York.

▲ When e-mails spread the "I love you" virus in May 2000, the Internet ground to a halt, and businesses lost billions of dollars. Investigators traced the attack to a 23-year-old Filipino man, Onel de Guzman, who created it for a college project. There is no law against making viruses in the Philippines, so de Guzman escaped prosecution.

Without leaving his desk in St. Petersburg, Russia, he electronically transferred more than $5 million into his own accounts. Detectives tracked him down by allowing him to continue his illegal transfers and tracing the money and phone calls back to Russia.

Such cases are very rare because banks now protect their central computers with more care. Today criminals find it easier to target online banking by "phishing"—sending out millions of spam e-mails (junk messages) to lure bank customers to fake web sites. These web sites often look exactly like an online bank, but they are completely fake. Customers are asked to enter their security codes and passwords. With this information, the criminals can then empty out that customer's account.

▼ Information sent on the Internet is not secure unless the browser page displays a tiny padlock symbol. Users who type in their credit card numbers on nonsecure pages risk having them stolen. Thieves then create fake credit cards with the same numbers and can run up huge bills.

Bombs and fires

Bombs and arson (deliberate fires) turn buildings and vehicles into charred ruins and rubble. Amazingly, though, even the fiercest blasts and flames do not burn up everything. Picking through the smoking embers, forensic experts often find enough of the device that triggered the destruction to trace it back to the criminals who placed it.

Dangerous flames

Buildings are designed to resist a blaze, so arsonists start their fires with accelerants—fast-burning fuels such as gasoline. To avoid being trapped in the fires themselves, some also use a timing device. An electric timer or even a candle resting on oil-soaked rags will delay the fire until the wick burns low.

A bigger bang

Bombs can be sophisticated or simple, but the results are usually the same—destruction and often death. The crudest bombs are made from low explosives. For example, even fertilizer and diesel fuel can make an explosive mixture.

Terrorists prefer high explosives such as Semtex—a handful is enough to blow up a car. Setting off any explosive is not as simple as it might seem. Most will not explode without detonators. Triggered by a timer these devices ignite with a tiny bang that then sets off the main charge.

◄ Despite the destruction that a terrorist car bomb causes, the pattern of damage can lead investigators to the location in the vehicle where the explosives were placed.

Investigation

Detectives investigating fires and bombs first need to find out what caused the destruction. A burst gas pipe, for example, could cause similar damage to that of a terrorist bomb.

To trace a fire's cause, detectives need to establish where it started. Often the only instruments they need are their eyes. Arson crime scenes may contain accelerants. To find small traces they use electronic "sniffers"—devices that detect them.

Patterns of soot and blast debris lead to the "seat" of the fire or explosion. This is where the destruction began, and it is there that investigators hope to find the device that lit the flames or triggered the explosion.

To identify the explosive or accelerant used at the crime scene, crime scene officers collect evidence in airtight containers. At the crime lab forensic scientists use microscopes to search the evidence for traces of explosives. They also run chemical tests on any vapor found inside the containers. Their instruments reveal the unique signatures of the chemicals that bombers and arsonists use.

◀ In suspicious fires police officers and firefighters work together to make buildings safe and check that everyone is accounted for. Then they block off the area to insure that only essential personnel work at the crime scene.

▼ A fingertip search at a bomb site can turn up traces of batteries, wires, and a timer. Comparing these traces with a computer database of similar devices from previous attacks puts police on the trail of the bomber.

Drugs and poisons

In thrilling true crime stories from the past cunning murderers slipped deadly powders into their victims' drinks. They also seemed to get away with it—but not anymore! This is because today's poisoners cannot beat the tests of toxicologists. These forensic specialists look for toxins—alcohol, drugs, and poisons—in human blood, urine, and flesh.

▲ Forensic testing kits change color when they are mixed with drugs. In this demonstration blue shows crack cocaine, black shows cannabis (marijuana), and red shows that amphetamines are present. Urine tests for drugs are much more sensitive than this because they must spot the tiny quantities that pass through a drug user's body.

▼ Mailed inside letters, the deadly bacteria anthrax killed three Americans in 2001. Scientists who studied the DNA of the germ discovered that it had been grown in a U.S. Army research center. Nobody was ever caught for the crime.

Sensitive tests

In the toxicology laboratory rows of machines process samples taken from suspects and corpses. These instruments can detect a drug diluted five billion times—the equivalent of two aspirin tablets dissolved in an Olympic-sized swimming pool. No wonder poisoners stand so little chance of avoiding detection! In fact, toxicologists hardly ever see poisons used as murder weapons anymore. Most cases of poisoning are accidents such as drug overdoses or people drinking weed killers by mistake.

▲ Poisoner Crippen was the first criminal to be caught by newly invented "wireless" radio. The captain of the ship on which he was traveling recognized him and radioed the Canadian police.

Looking for drugs

Toxicologists work on samples of body fluid or organs, such as the liver, that are removed during an autopsy. But not all of the samples are from dead subjects. Toxicologists also work with the police to stop people from using illegal drugs. Police officers carry out simple tests when an arrest is made. A five-minute "dip and read" urine-testing kit changes in pattern or color if it is likely that an illegal drug is present. If this test shows a "yes" result, a nurse would take a blood sample for further testing in the lab.

Two-stage tests

In the lab testing is done in two stages. The first stage makes sure that the sample contains drugs; a second test figures out the exact amount. In modern labs toxicologists use testing machines like small robots. These suck up the samples, prepare them, run the tests, and then present the results on a computer screen. This technology is vital in alcohol testing. Analyzing samples from drunk drivers makes up most of the work of a toxicology lab, and testing by hand would take much too long.

Catching Doctor Crippen

When Doctor Hawley Crippen (1862–1910) announced that his unfaithful wife had left London, England, to return to the U.S., her friends became suspicious. After Crippen himself vanished police dug up the basement of his house and found his wife's body. Tests showed a lethal dose of the drug hyoscine. Crippen was spotted on an Atlantic cruise ship, with his attractive secretary disguised as a boy. The couple was arrested on their arrival in Canada, and Crippen was hung for murder four months later.

▶ Police found this bag of heroin when they raided a drug dealer's apartment. Toxicologists are more likely to come across the drug when addicts take too much of it. It shows up in the blood, hair, and organ tissue of those who die from an overdose.

▶ Easy detection stops murderers from using poison, but terrorists do not fear discovery. They use poison to cause panic and disruption. Terrorists succeeded in 2004 when a poison scare shut down most of the U.S. Congress. U.S. Marines wore protective suits to check for ricin, a deadly nerve poison, that was sent to an American politician.

Weapons

In a murder investigation finding a weapon brings the detectives on the case one step closer to the killer. Although knives and clubs rarely leave identifying marks on victims, guns provide detectives with more useful evidence. Spiral ridges found inside the barrel of a gun, known as rifling, mark bullets with grooves that are as distinctive as fingerprints. Pulling the trigger stains the killer's hands, also making identification easier.

▲ By test firing a gun from different distances, firearms experts can estimate how far apart a killer and the victim were. At close range a gun leaves a bigger deposit of gunpowder around the wound.

▶ Crime scene officers handle firearms with great care—not just to preserve evidence but also because guns are deadly when they are loaded. Here an investigator makes a gun safe by removing the magazine of bullets. She wears gloves in order to avoid putting her own fingerprints on the weapon.

Which gun fired the fatal shot?

From a bullet's shape firearms examiners—forensic experts who specialize in guns and their use—can guess *what* type of gun fired it. But finding out exactly *which* gun is more difficult. This is done by looking at the grooves on the bullet's surface that are caused by rifling. These ridges, found in the gun's barrel, spin the bullet in order to keep its flight straight.

Matching bullet and gun

The rifling marks have more value as evidence if investigators find a suspect's gun. To judge whether this gun shot the fatal bullet, they load and fire it.

▲ The U.S. *Brasscatcher* database records images of cartridge cases from guns used in crimes. If a cartridge case from a new crime matches one on the database, this means that the same gun has been used again.

New crime scene kits allow police to wipe a suspect's hands with a swab soaked in a special chemical and immediately see if they have fired a gun recently.

◀ In a gun test by U.S. police a firearms examiner aims the weapon safely into a water tank. Comparison of the bullet with those found at the crime scene will show whether the suspect fired this gun.

Dirty hands

Guns leave another type of mark that is extremely useful to detectives when tracking killers. A small amount of the explosive in the cartridge case always sprays out from gaps in the gun's mechanism. This is called gunshot residue. Some of this residue will end up on the gunman's hands. So testing a suspect's hands for gunshot residue can prove that they fired a gun in the previous six hours.

Catching the bullet safely in water or soft material preserves the telltale grooves. A comparison microscope allows the firearms examiner to see whether the marks match those found on the bullet taken from the victim's body.

When there is no suspect weapon, firearms examiners may see if the grooves match those grooves found on bullets fired in previous crimes. They do this using a computer program that stores and compares rifling marks.

Cartridge cases

Bullets are not the only useful type of firearms evidence. For each bullet fired there is also a cartridge case. This metal tube contains the explosive charge that propels the bullet forward. Pulling a gun's trigger forces a hammer onto the end of the cartridge, detonating the explosive inside. The hammer leaves a mark as distinctive as the groove on the bullet, and this can be matched in a similar way.

Most guns eject a cartridge case each time they are fired. Where these cases fall can help detectives figure out where the suspect was standing when they pulled the trigger (see page 15).

▼ Shotgun pellets spread as they fly from the barrel. The size of the pattern they form shows the distance between the gun and target. This X-ray shows the result of a close-range shooting.

Fakes and forgeries

They look like $20 bills. They feel like money, and they are printed on thick, crisp paper like all U.S. bills. But forged or fake paper money is worthless. Worse, you could face jail if you spend it. Money is the oldest and easiest target for forgers, but today these criminals are as likely to copy valuable documents, art, credit cards, DVDs, watches, or even designer clothes.

Trademark pirates

Dior, Nike, Rolex, Adidas, Prada—designer labels stand for quality and style, but how can you be sure that what you are wearing is the real thing? Forgers are making a fortune by selling us bogus goods that look just like the brands that they imitate.

▼ The pirate DVDs these soldiers are destroying in Ecuador sell for a fraction of the cost of the real thing. The poor-quality recordings do not deter customers who buy nine fakes for each genuine disc sold.

◄ Passport fraud is a big business, but making a passport that looks genuine is not easy. More often forgers buy stolen passports and change the photo and name to those of the person who is buying one.

Cheats at the register

People are less easily fooled than the machines, although very good forged bills are difficult to tell apart from the real thing. To recognize the counterfeits, document examiners (forensic forgery specialists) use microscopes and chemical tests. Tracing the type and source of the paper and ink may lead them to the forgers. By plotting where criminals used identical bills, they can follow the progress of the gang, which should hopefully lead to their arrest.

Fashion victims

Detecting fake designer goods becomes more and more difficult as forgers become more clever. When antipiracy detectives swoop in on clothing factories, they now take with them fashion industry experts to examine every stitch. Clothing companies are helping too, with hard-to-forge labels and hidden security features that can only be spotted if you know where to look. But as long as people crave the look without the price, the trade seems certain to continue.

Printing money

Money is very different from clothes. Nobody wants a fake bill in their wallet, so banks try hard to make their bills impossible to copy. They use tiny printing, special inks, foil strips, holograms, and watermarks—images built into the paper that appear only when you hold the bill up to the light.

Nevertheless, forgers still copy money using many different printing methods and papers. None exactly matches the special printing presses that banks use, although some come close. Color photocopies were good enough to fool change-making machines, until the bills and machines were altered to catch the fakes.

▼ In the chaos that wars cause forgers thrive. U.S. soldiers found these sheets of uncut bills when they invaded Iraq in 2003. The criminals who printed them hoped to pass them off as real when Iraq's banks changed over to new bills later in the year.

Not so fantastic plastic

Plastic debit and credit cards are easier to forge than money because each bank uses different patterns—while every $20 bill looks exactly the same. Criminals constantly search for ways to defeat card security features. For example, dishonest workers in stores and restaurants swipe genuine cards through a pocket-sized card reader in order to steal security details from the magnetic strips. Recording the same data onto fake cards ensures that they are accepted at the register.

To combat card crime, document examiners look for links between cards such as a tiny fault in the embossed name. This enables them to identify cards made by the same forgers.

Bogus masterpiece

Faking the work of a famous painter is tougher than forging a credit card. To make pictures that will fool art experts, forgers must copy not only artists' styles but also their materials. Modern paints are very different from those

▲ To test whether an "old" painting really is genuine, scientists need to remove only the tiniest flecks of paint. Studying the paint using special techniques, such as mass spectroscopy and infrared spectroscopy, may reveal what it is made from.

that artists used 100 years ago, so analyzing paint can reveal a painting's age.

Although a convincing fake can sell for millions of dollars, not all art forgeries get such high prices. Because of the difficulty of faking the work of great artists, many art forgers tackle easier projects. They make cheaper artworks that experts will not study as closely. For example, as many as half of all "ancient" Greek bronze statues are probably fake since they are easy to make. They sell well to private collectors, who are less likely to notice a fake than the staff of galleries who have access to instruments to verify the materials used.

◄ English forger Tom Keating (1918–1984) tricked the art world by painting hundreds of fakes. Some still hang undetected on gallery walls. Keating did not do it for the money. A failed artist, he turned to forgery to get his revenge against the critics who disliked his paintings.

SUMMARY OF CHAPTER 3: CRIME LAB

The need for a laboratory

A lot of the forensic scientist's work is done in a laboratory. One of the most important tasks there is to examine the bodies of people who have died in suspicious circumstances. During autopsies forensic pathologists look closely at the outsides of bodies and then cut them open to study their organs, flesh, and fluids.

What happens at the laboratory?

Forensic scientists study trace evidence left behind by criminals. Crime scene officers collect traces with tape or special vacuum cleaners and examine them under a microscope. The natural world is a good source of useful trace evidence. Soil, plants, and insects found on corpses can tell scientists a lot about the crime committed.

Computer software and hardware is used to find evidence stored electronically. Scientists target traditional criminals or hackers who spread havoc online.

Other forensic scientists specialize in fire and explosions. Experts sift evidence from scenes of devastation to see what fueled the blast or flames.

They search for traces of a timing device that might hold vital clues about the identity of who started the fire.

In the laboratory toxicologists test body fluids for evidence of drug abuse or poison. A lot of their work aims to prove the guilt of drunk drivers.

If guns are found, specialist firearms examiners are called in. They fire seized guns and compare the bullets with those found at the crime scene. Marks and scratches can show if the same gun was used in the crime. Cartridge cases also carry marks that can tell a similar story. Gunshot residue on criminals' hands may prove that they pulled the trigger.

Pollen grains can provide clues for forensic scientists

Go further . . .

Find out how dental records can help identify a victim at: www.cyberbee.com/ whodunnit/teeth.html

Become a forensic scientist and use chemistry to help identify the mysterious white powder at: www.cyberbee.com/whodunnit/ powder.html

Discover how to find any hidden files on your computer by visiting: www.whyfiles.org/014forensic/ computer_data.html

KFK Mummies, by John Malam (Kingfisher, 2003)

Document examiner
Examines suspicious documents for changes, decides whether they are genuine or fake, and compares handwriting and signatures.

Electronic caseworker
Unravels the information stored in suspects' computers, handheld organizers, and cell phones.

Firearms examiner
Checks, tests, and compares weapons and ammunition used in crimes and analyzes evidence to find out how suspects used their guns.

Toxicologist
Tests body fluids and tissues for traces of drugs and alcohol.

Use forensic techniques to identify fingerprints, footprints, DNA, and hair samples to solve a crime:
Thinktank
Birmingham, England B4 7XG
Phone: +44 0 121 202 2222
www.thinktank.ac.uk

Visit "Whodunit: The Science of Solving Crime" exhibition at:
Museum of Discovery and Science
401 SW. Second Street
Fort Lauderdale, FL 33312
Phone: (954) 467-6637
http://www.mods.org

Glossary

assassin
A murderer—especially one who attacks by surprise.

bacteria
Tiny living things, some of which cause diseases in animals or plants.

barrel of a gun
The tube-shaped front end of a gun that guides a bullet toward its target.

blackmailer
Someone who has information that will damage their victim and who demands money to keep it a secret.

body bag
A zip-up bag for carrying a dead body and preserving evidence clinging to it.

cartridge case
The brass cap that holds together a bullet and the explosive charge needed to fire it.

CCTV
Short for closed-circuit television—a security camera.

chain of custody
A list of all the people who have handled a piece of evidence between the crime scene and the court.

chain of proof
A series of linked facts or evidence.

corpse
A dead body.

court
The place where a trial is held.

crime scene officer
An investigator who works at the scene of a crime.

cross section
The shape of something when it is cut in half.

crowbar
A hooked metal bar used for prying things open.

database
A computerized list.

dental charts
A chart showing the condition of each one of a person's teeth.

DFO
Short for 1,8-diaza-9-fluorenone, a chemical that makes fingerprints on paper glow.

"dip and read" urine test
A testing strip that changes color when it is dipped in urine if the person has recently taken a drug or if there is glucose or blood present.

drug
A medicine or chemical sometimes used illegally to create an altered state of consciousness.

evidence
An object, a mark, or information that tells investigators about a crime.

evidence card
A piece of cardboard to which detectives stick evidence such as fingerprints.

explosion
The blast caused by a bomb or the uncontrolled burning of gas or fuel.

FBI
Short for Federal Bureau of Investigation—the national detective agency of the U.S.

fiber
A strand of thread.

fingertip search
A very detailed search in which detectives run their hands over an area to check for evidence.

genes
Patterns of simple chemicals that control the shape and growth of every living thing. Parents pass on genes to their children.

guilty
To be blamed for a crime.

hacker
Someone who breaks into a computer system and changes or steals computer data, either to commit a crime or to create havoc.

innocent
Not to be blamed for a crime. *See also* guilty.

judge
An official who is in charge of a court and who decides how a criminal should be punished.

jury
A group of ordinary people who listen to evidence at a trial and decide whether a suspect is guilty or innocent.

lie detector
The nickname for a polygraph, a device used to measure changes in a suspect's sweating, breathing, and heartbeat when they give untrue answers to questions.

light-bending power
The ability of a transparent substance, such as glass, to bend a beam of light passing through it.

magnetic brush
A brush containing a magnet for dusting fingerprints with iron powder without actually touching them.

mug shot
Slang for an identity photograph—usually of a criminal.

online
Connected or provided through the Internet.

pathologist
A medical doctor who studies diseases and injuries and their causes.

pattern evidence
Any type of evidence where the objects or marks themselves are less important than the pattern that they form.

piracy
Robbery at sea, but now used to mean the copying of someone's work or of a company's products.

police lineup
A chance for a witness to pick out a suspect from similar-looking people.

pulse
The throbbing in someone's veins and arteries caused by the heart's pumping action.

rifling
Spiraling ridges cut inside a gun's barrel. Rifling spins bullets, making them hit the target more accurately.

scale
An object, such as a ruler, with marks a set distance apart, to make size and distance more obvious.

scalpel
A very sharp knife used by surgeons.

spam
Unwanted "junk" e-mail, often containing a hidden program that can damage the computer it runs on.

suspect
Someone whom investigators believe might be to blame for a crime.

suspicious death
Any death that police believe may have been caused by a criminal act such as murder.

trial
The process of deciding whether or not a suspect is guilty and—if they are—how they should be punished.

ultraviolet radiation
An invisible form of energy similar to light.

vital signs
Signs such as warmth and a pulse that show that someone is alive.

VMD
Short for vacuum metal deposition, a way of making fingerprints show up on shiny surfaces such as plastic.

Index

Acknowledgments

The publisher would like to thank the following for permission to reproduce their material. Every care has been taken to trace copyright holders. However, if there have been unintentional omissions or failure to trace copyright holders, we apologize and will, if informed, endeavor to make corrections in any future edition.

Key: *b* = bottom, *c* = center, *l* = left, *r* = right, *t* = top

Cover *left* Science Photo Library (SPL)/Michael Donne; cover *center background* SPL/Mehau Kulyk; cover *center foreground* SPL/Mehau Kulyk; cover *right* SPL/Tek Image; page 1 Corbis/Reuters; 2–3 Corbis/Ron Sachs; 4–5 Getty News; 7 Getty Stone; 8–9 Alamy/Wesley Hitt; 8*bl* Corbis/Mark Peterson; 9*tr* Getty News; 9*br* Getty Stone; 10–11 Alamy/Shout; 10*tr* Getty Stone; 11*br* Corbis/Reuters; 12*bl* Associated Press; 12*cr* SPL/Michael Donne; 13 SPL/Michael Donne; 14*tr* Alamy/Plainpicture; 14*b* Alamy/Carphoto; 15*bl* Getty News; 15 Getty Stone; 16–17 Corbis/Mark Peterson; 16*bl* SPL/Pascal Goetgheluck; 17*tr* SPL/Alfred Pasieka; 18*t* Alamy/Imagesource; 18*tr* SPL/Volker Steger; 18*b* Alamy/Comstock; 19 Alamy/JG Photography; 19*b* Alamy/Mikael Karlsson; 20*bl* SPL/Volker Steger; 20*r* Getty; 21*br* Corbis/Charles O'Rear; 22 Rex Features; 23 Digital Vision; 24–25 SPL/Andrew Syred; 24*bl* Corbis; 24–25*c* Corbis/Robert Patrick; 25*tr* SPL/Eurelios; 25*b* SPL/Peter Menzel; 26–27 Imaging Body; 26*tr* Getty Photographer's Choice; 26*b* SPL/Tek Image; 27*br* SPL/Colin Cuthbert; 28–29 Corbis; 28*tr* Alamy/Pat Behnke; 28*bl* Getty/Photographer's Choice; 28*br* Corbis; 29*t* Alamy; 29*b* SPL/Mauro Fermariello; 30*l* Corbis/Sygma; 30*cr* SPL/Mauro Fermariello; 30*br* SPL/Michel Viard; 31*b* SPL/John McClean; 32 SPL/Mauro Fermariello; 32–33 Corbis; 33*tl* Corbis/Reuters; 33*b* SPL/Philippe Plailly; 34*l* Alamy; 35*t* Corbis/Reuters; 35*b* Corbis/Sygma; 36*l* Corbis/Reuters; 36–37*c* Corbis/Reuters; 37*r* Alamy/Brand X; 38 SPL/Peter Menzel; 39 SPL/Volker Steger; 40–41 Corbis/San Francisco Chronicle; 41*tr* SPL/Custom Medical Stock; 43 SPL/Gca; 44–45 SPL/Eye of Science; 44*tl* SPL/David Scarf; 44*tcl* SPL/Eye of Science; 44*bcl* SPL/Eye of Science; 44*bl* SPL/Eye of Science; 44*br* SPL/Mauro Fermariello; 45*tr* SPL/Mauro Fermariello; 45*bl* Alamy/Mikael Karlsson; 46–47*t* SPL/Pascal Goetgheluck; 46*tl* PL/Volker Steger; 47*br* SPL/Susumu Nishinaga; 48–49 Getty Imagebank; 48*tr* Alamy; 49*t* Corbis/Sygma; 49*br* Alamy/Comstock; 50–51 SPL/Michael Donne; 50*cl* Corbis/Francois de Mulder; 50–51*b* Alamy/Blue Shadows; 51*r* Associated Press; 52–53 Corbis; 52*tl* SPL/Mauro Fermariello; 52*cr* Getty News; 52*bl* Corbis/CDC; 53*tr* SPL/Gusto; 53*b* Corbis/Reuters; 54*tr* Alamy/Mikael Karlsson; 54*bl* SPL/Mauro Fermariello; 54*br* Getty News; 55*tl* Getty News; 55*tr* Getty News; 55*b* SPL/ISM; 56–57 Corbis/Sygma; 56 Getty News; 57*tl* Getty News; 57*b* Getty News; 58 SPL/Andrew Syred; 58*tr* SPL/Volker Steger; 58*b* Rex Features; 60*l* Imaging Body; 62–63 Rex Features; 64 Corbis/Reuters

The publisher would like to thank the following illustrators:
34–35*tr* Encompass Graphics; 42–43*r* Jurgen Ziewe